CONTENTS

1:00 WHAT THIS BOOK IS ALL ABOUT AND WHY I HAVE WRITTEN IT..................2

2:00 INTRODUCTION..................6

3:00 THINGS YOU A CHRISTIAN NEEDS TO KNOW ABOUT BUSINESS AND BEING IN BUSINESS..................20

4:00 BASIC FACTORS RELATING TO BUSINESS SUCCESS WHICH YOU A CHRISTIAN MUST KNOW BEFORE STARTING YOUR OWN BUSINESS..................36

5:00 THINGS YOU A CHRISTIAN MUST DO TO BE ABLE TO FIND AND SELECT A BUSINESS YOU CAN START..................44

6:00 HOW YOU A CHRISTIAN CAN CREATE A SUCCESSFUL BUSINESS 64

APPENDIX:A BUSINESS PLAN TEMPLATE...75

1:00 WHAT THIS BOOK IS ALL ABOUT AND WHY I HAVE WRITTEN IT

This book discusses and explains what business should be to a Christian and how a Christian can find, select and create a business.

It also discusses how a Christian in business should run his business.

My main objective for writing this book is to explain to Christians what business should be to them and how they should see and do it. I have had to write the book because in the course of my interaction with Christians, in the church and the marketplace I discovered that most Christians are ignorant of what business really is and how they as Christians should see and do business.

I discovered that because most Christians do not know what business should really be to a Christian they see, define and do business just as the people of the world. It is because of this that those who go into business fail and they are unable to be the light that they are supposed to be in the marketplace.

It is my desire that this book which you are holding in your hand will bring a change to this situation that Christians are in through educating them about business so that they know what business really is to a Christian, how a Christian should see business and how a Christian should do business.

This book has therefore been written to enlighten and encourage Christians to not only go into business and do it as Christians but to see business as a Christian calling.

It is with the prayer that this book serves this purpose of educating you a Christian about business and encouraging you to see business for what it is to a Christian that I commit it into your hands.

2:00 INTRODUCTION

Most Christians who wants to start businesses of their own think finding and starting a business is all about ,

(a) Finding a business opportunity

(b) Acquiring the skills needed to produce the product or render the service that meets the need that the business opportunity reveals

(c) Acquiring the financial capital to secure,

(i) the equipment

(ii) raw materials needed for producing the product.

(iii) pay the rent for the premises/offices.

Experience has however revealed that for a person to be able to find, select, create and run a business successfully there are more things he needs to address than those listed above.

This book provides you a Christian, who would want to find and start a business of your own with an explanation of the things that you a Christian must know and be able to do to succeed in a business you start.

For you a Christian who would want to start a business of your own, you must and should know these things and be able to do them or find other Christians who can do them and are willing to partner with you before you commit your savings and indeed your future on a business idea which you think can launch you into a business of your own.

Follow me to the remaining chapters of this book where I have discussed and explained in details these things that you a Christian needs to know and be able to do to find and start a business of your own.

I have also explained how you a Christian can acquire these things that you should have to be able to do what you need to do to find, start and succeed in a business of your own.

WHAT IS A BUSINESS?

To most people business is all about making money and so a business is anything a person does to get money. It is because of this that business and doing business to most people is all about making money and money alone.

To this people once an activity enables them to get money then it is a business.

For a Christian this is not and should not be what a business is. From what we read in the Bible, the manual of life , this is not the way God intends that business should be and so this is not the definition of business especially for those who are Christians. Christians should therefore not see and do business only as a money making activity.

From what we read in the Bible, business as God intends it to be especially for a Christian is, an endeavor which enables a Christian who engages in it to be able to live and be who he has been called to be and fulfill the purpose that he has been created for.

Business is therefore any endeavor which enables a person to live and through doing it achieve the following three things which living should be about for Christians because of who they really are on earth.

(i) Become who he has been called to be.

Every Christian has been called to be disciple of Jesus Christ.

This means every Christian should seek to become like Christ in character. What a Christian does as his business(Life endeavor) should amongst other things be a means of training for him to become like Christ.

Only Jesus has ever lived and fulfilled His life purpose fully on earth hence God desires that we become like Him.

It is because of this that He works through all that comes our way to make us become like Him and He also wants us through what we do as our businesses(Life endeavors) to be trained to become like Christ .

(ii)CREATE VALUE THAT MEETS A NEED OR SOLVES A PROBLEM FOR OTHERS.

Every Christian has been called to be a servant and so what a Christian does as business must enable him to be able to serve others through value creation that meets a need they have.

A Christians business should be an avenue for producing products or rendering services that benefits and improves others and the environment.

An activity that enables a person to do this satisfies the fact that every human life has been created and is in the world as a solution to a human problem and so it should be lived for solving human problems. It is because of this that it is usually said that every human being is an answer to some ones prayer for the solution of a human problem.

(iii) GENERATES RESOURCES HE NEEDS TO MEET HIS NEEDS AND BE SUSTAINED.

A Christian needs resources to meet his physical needs for sustenance. Prominent amongst these resources that a Christian needs for sustenance and can get as he does his business is money. A business should help a Christian to make money.

(iv) BE A WITNESS FOR CHRIST

Every Christian has been called to be a witness for Christ in the world and so a Christian's business must enable such a Christian to be a witness for Christ as he relates to people and serves them.

These four things are the things that, what a Christian does as business must help him to do and achieve.

If an endeavor does not enable a Christian to achieve these four things then it is not a business a Christian can be involved in.

From Genesis 1:28 which says," God blessed them and said to them, "Be fruitful and increase in number; fill the earth and subdue it. Rule over the fish of the sea and the birds of the air and over every living creature that moves on the ground." We can bring out things that make up the criteria that an activity that a Christian can do as a business must meet.

From this verse we can see that, the criteria that an activity must meet for it to be a business for a Christian are,

(i) It must be an activity God can bless

(ii) It must have fruit, it produces a product or render a service that benefits people, meet a need they have.

(iii) It must solve a human problem

(iv) It must be an avenue to produce others

(v) It must enable a person to dominate an area of life.

It is because every human being has been created and is in the world as a solution to a human problem that it is usually said, " every human being is an answer to some ones prayer for the solution of a human problem".

For us to understand why business should be seen and done by Christians as I have described above we will need to go back to the book of beginnings, GENESIS and see why God created man and how He intended him to live and fulfill the purpose for which he has been created.

From Genesis 1:26 which says,

Then God said, "Let us make man in our image, in our likeness, and let them rule over the fish of the sea and the birds of the air, over the livestock, over all the earth, and over all the creatures that move along the ground."

we see why God created man and in Genesis 1:28 which says ,God blessed them and said to them, "Be fruitful and increase in number; fill the earth and subdue it. Rule over the fish of the sea and the birds of the air and over every living creature that moves on the ground." we see how God intended for man to live and be able to fulfill the purpose for which he has been created.

Genesis 1:28 is mans mandate, it is clear about the fact that it can be fulfilled only through man being fruitful. Work enables man to be fruitful, hence in Genesis 2:15 we read, The Lord God took the man and put him in the Garden of Eden to work it and take care of it.

God gave man work as the means for the fulfillment of this mandate. An endeavor that can serve as a business must therefore enable a person to work and achieve all the things I discussed above.

Despite the fall of man, his mandate and how it is to be fulfilled has not changed. The only thing that has come in as additional requirement for man to be able to live and fulfill his purpose which work as God design it is still relevant and the means to fulfill purpose is the aspect of it enabling man to become like Christ. Doing business which enables people to work is able to serve this need of transforming them and so the definition of business has not change despite the fall.

From what I have discussed above it is clear that business is not and should not be a money making activity only. A person's business is his life endeavor and it should help the person to be able to live out his life purpose.

3:00 THINGS YOU A CHRISTIAN NEEDS TO KNOW ABOUT BUSINESS AND BEING IN BUSINESS

Finding, starting, creating and being in business by you a Christian will entail a very different way of living life for you as compared with you finding a job and being an employee.

Studies have revealed that being in business of your own will bring into your life many things that a person who is an employee will not experience or face.

This means for you a Christian who wants to go into a business of your own, you will right from the start have to prepare yourself to adapt and live by a different lifestyle from that of an employee.

There are therefore things that you a Christian, who wants to go into a business of your own will need to know right from the start about business and being in business before you start.

Prominent amongst these things are,

what business really is for you a Christian.

what being in business and doing business is all about for you a Christian.

what being in business will mean to you and how being in business will affect you as a person.

(a) WHAT BUSINESS IS FOR YOU A CHRISTIAN

For you a Christian who is going into a business of your own, you will need to know what business is to be to you.

Studies have revealed that the ultimate goal of a business is value creation for people. It is about finding and solving a human problem or meeting a human need and since you can do this only with a product or a service, being in business for you a Christian will entail you will be producing and trading a product or service.

(b) WHAT BEING IN BUSINESS IS ALL ABOUT FOR YOU AS A PERSON

Because of what business is, being in a business of your own will mean the following to you as a person,

(i) GREATER FREEDOM:

You will have greater freedom about how you work, this is especially so if you are moving from regular employment e.g. public service

(ii) MORE RESPONSIBILITY:

(a) The buck stops with you, you call all the shots, you make the decisions and own up to them. You own the risks.

(b) If you are moving from being an employee to starting your own business, you will need to know that, being in business will mean you have virtually exchanged your dependence for independence and inter-dependence (with others e.g. customers, suppliers, bankers, government officials etc).

Your ability to successfully manage these dependence and inter-dependence is a critical success factor in your business.

(iii) BUSINESS CAN BECOMES PART OF YOUR EGO:

Many in business have associated who they are to their business and so success in business builds up their ego, while failure damages their ego (some people who have failed in business have committed suicide). People stake their person on their businesses so for you a Christian you will need to stake your identity and success on God not your business.

Being able to do this will enable you to depend on God in running the business.

(iv) UNCERTAINTY:

Being in your own business will mean everything is uncertain and so living by faith and coping with the unknown will become a key aspect of being in business of your own.

(v) HOLISTICNESS

Tasks are performed in a holistic nature i.e. you are the person running all the show, unlike in regular employment where you do your own part and leave the rest to others. Now as a self employed person, your decisions are done in form of holistic tasks.

(vi) CUSTOMER-BASED REWARDS:

Your lifestyle is now dependent on how successful you are with the customer. If the customer refuses to buy, then you do not have any income and this will definitely affect your life style.

(vii) NETWORKING:

To succeed in business you will need others and you may have to do away with others and as such you will have to pay attention to relationships. Building of new relationships and the review of existing ones will be necessary – new friends, new partners etc may be necessary. You may have to give up some old friends because of your new work schedule.

(viii) INTEGRATION OF, SPIRITUAL, SOCIAL AND BUSINESS LIFE:

Your spiritual, social and family life become more fused into your business life. The dividing line gets thinner and hence there is need for caution.

(ix) LONG AND VARIABLE HOURS OF WORK:

You may be required to work very long hours and sometimes at "unreasonable" times (compared to conventional work hours). This will seriously impact on your life, at times with undesired consequences to family life. There is therefore need for balance and understanding to be reached between you and members of your family on this.

(x) OWNERSHIP AND RISK:

You may have to put some money and family assets at risk if you are in business. This is different from life in regular employment.

(xi) LEARNING:

As you start out in your business, one of the new aspects of your life is that, you will have to learn new things every day. Hardly anything in business is routine, unlike in regular employment where many things are routine. You will also need to learn from mistakes, experiments, actions and feedback. You will have to use these to build lessons into your business.

(xii) VULNERABLE:

Because you are small and new to the business environment when you start, you are vulnerable to people and events. You will need to depend on God be alert and realistic of the business world and constantly think strategically to cope with the changes, pressures and problems that may occur.

Apart from the above things which have to do with how being in business will affect you as a person, there are also things you must know and be able to do before you consider opening the doors of your business.

Prominent amongst these things are,

(i) You must know your product or service.

Many people are in business but they do not know their product or service and as such they are unable to sell it well. You must therefore know what your product or service really is before you open your doors. Failure to know what your business product or service really is will result in you not knowing how to sell it and who to sell it to. You must therefore know your product or service before you open the doors of your business.

You must know what your product or service really is and how to produce or render it as best as you can. You should know this better than anyone is presently doing it before you consider opening your doors. This will give you an edge over your competitors and the staff you will employ to work with you will not cheat you.

Please note that when I speak of you having the knowledge of your product or service I am not talking of you just knowing what it is called; I am talking of you knowing what the product or service is called and what it does to people and why people want it. Having this knowledge will enable you know how best to produce and serve the product or service. It is even better if you do not only know how to produce the product or provide the service but you have a practical experience in producing the product or rendering the service.

(ii)Legal status acquisition

You will need to know all the legal requirements for the business you want to start and where you can secure them. These may be permits licenses etc. Knowing these and acquiring them is necessary and a very important requirement for the existence and survival of your business. This means before you open your doors you must make sure that your business is registered with the appropriate Government agencies and you have or know where to acquire all the licenses that you need to produce and sell your product or service.

You must and should not be involved in doing anything illegally.

It is said that the law has a long arm, this is very true as you cannot escape the law. The law will sooner than you expect catches up with you so do not cut corners when it comes to legal matters.

(iii) systems

To produce and sell a product or service you will need **systems.** A business produces and sells products or services and hence it needs to have systems. For your business to succeed it must have well defined and effective systems. You must therefore know, define very clearly and design the systems you need for your business to operate successfully before you open your doors.

Your business systems are the processes you must follow to produce your product or render your service. You will need to know them and how to establish and run them effectively and efficiently for the operations in your business to produce your product or render your service efficiently effectively and profitably.

(iv) Effective communication

This has to do with reaching out and talking with those who will be involved with you in your business.

These will include those who will work with you within and without your business. Communication both within and without a business impacts the cash flow of a business hence it is a vital requirement for the success of a business

Communication without a business has to do with communication with its customers; it is often called public relations, marketing, advertising and sales. Communication within a business has to do with communication with its workers, suppliers, management and shareholders. You must therefore have an effective way of communication for your business before you open your doors.

(v)cash flow

The cash flow of a business is about the flow of money into and out of a business. Money to a business is like blood to a human being and as such it's flow into and out of a business must be such that it remains positive always or else the business will die for lack of money as a man who lacks blood dies.

You will need to know the kind of financial records a business must keep to be able to manage its finances well so that you manage your finances well. You must know how this is done and you do it because without maintaining correct and up to date financial records your business will not survive.

(For a detail explanation of what books and records a business should keep and how to keep them you can refer to my book titled,

"HOW TO KEEP FINANCIAL RECORDS FOR YOUR SMALL BUSINESS")

4:00 BASIC REQUIREMENTS FOR BUSINESS SUCCESS WHICH YOU MUST KNOW AND HAVE BEFORE STARTING YOUR OWN BUSINESS

For you to succeed in your business when you start, there are things that you must know and have. These things that you must know and have are what I call the basic requirements for success in a business.

These things make up the foundational requirements for success in an endeavor.

Studies have revealed that people fail in endeavors they embark on because they do not know and acquire these foundational requirements before they start.

Most people are ignorant of this fact that there are basic foundational requirements for success in an endeavor which a person must acquire before he embarks on an endeavor and as such they embark on endeavors without first acquiring them and they end up failing.

This means that for a person to be able to succeed in an endeavor he must and should first become a person who can carry out successfully the activities that must be carried out for the endeavor to be said to have been successful executed. This is because a person is said to have carried out an endeavor successfully only if he is able to carry out the activities that must be done for the endeavor to be achieved successfully and the purpose for the execution of the endeavor is achieved.

The above fact is saying that, for you a Christian to be able to start a business and succeed in it, you will first need to know what these foundational requirements are for business and acquire them before you start. Failure to do this will result in failure.

Studies have revealed that these foundational requirements for success in an endeavor which you wanting to start a business must have to be able to go into business and succeed are,

(i) commitment to do business

(ii) competence to do business

(iii) capacity to do business

EXPLANATIONS OF THE FOUNDATIONAL REQUIREMENTS FOR SUCCESS IN BUSINESS

Commitment

The dictionary defines the word commitment as being loyal to or to be dedicated to.

This is a product of conviction and perception.

A person who wants to go into a business of his own will need to be committed to it to succeed. It has however been discovered that he will be committed to the business he starts if he is convicted about being in business and he has the right perception about business and being in business.

Having the conviction and the right perception about business and to be in business and be committed is a product of having the right knowledge of what business and being in business is all about .

Having this knowledge will enable a person to be able to know the true meaning of business and what business is all about(the purpose of business) Such a person will have a good reason for being in business and can go out and do what it takes to find, select, create and be in business and remain in such a business come rain come shine.

Competence

Competence is ability to do, it is simply called skill.

For a person to be able to carry out an endeavor well he must have the skills sets needed for success in an endeavor. Studies have revealed that there are two skills sets needed for every endeavor. They are micro and macro skills.

For you a Christian going into business you must make sure you have the micro skill which is the craft skill for the business you are going into and the macro skills which are the personal attributes you need to be able to use your micro skills well.

Capacity

Capacity can simply be defined as the inner strength and grace to be able to withstand the pressures that will come on a person when engaged in an endeavor.

It is a function of character.

For you to be able to find, select, create and run successfully the business you start you will need the character to be able to withstand the pressures you will be exposed to by the business you do and the money you will make.

5:00 WHAT YOU A CHRISTIAN SHOULD DO TO BE ABLE TO FIND AND SELECT A BUSINESS YOU CAN START.

Business is a channel for service and a means for making (developing) a person. It is the means through which a person can serve others using the talents and gifts he has been equipped with and through doing that, become who he has been created to become and do what he has been created to do in the world well.

This means, for a Christian to be able to find, select and start a business to do and be able to achieve these things mentioned above he will need to know and find some things.

Prominent amongst these things that,

(a) he must know, is his life purpose and what his talents and gifts are.

He will need to know his purpose in life, talents and gifts. He will also need to know what he can do with them. For details of how to discover your life purpose, please refer to the author's book titled, **YOU AND YOUR LIFE.**

(b) He must have is a business opportunity.

To enable him find the business he can do successfully with the talents and gifts he has to fulfill his life purpose, he will need to find a business **IDEA** which is a **BUSINESS OPPORTUNITY**.

A business opportunity is a business idea that has a big enough market to sustain its implementation. He can then create an enterprise with which he can use the idea he found to produce a product or service which satisfy the human need or solve the human problem which the opportunity he found reveals.

In addition to the things that you must know and have is a major activity which you must do to be able to find and select a business you can start.

Doing this activity will not only enable you to know if you as a person is ready for doing business but it will also enable you to find and select a business that will be right for you (fits you) and you will enjoy doing when you start.

This activity which you must carry out is made up of the following activities,

(a) SELF APPRAISAL

Being the pivot on which the business revolves, there is need for an objective self-appraisal to know who you really are by identifying your areas of strengths and weaknesses. Carrying out this appraisal will assist you in your decision to go into business of your own.

To asses oneself is not easy, however if you are one of those who can have a difficulty in undertaking this exercise you can ask a colleague to help. Below are some basic sample questions that could assist you in carrying out the exercise objectively (you can come up with others which can help in enabling you know who you really are)

* What do people think of me?

* What do I think of myself?

*   Is the business project the type that has long hours and much stress?

*   Am I ready to sacrifice my leisure time to face the business?

*   How do I rate my business capacity?

*   Do I have experience in the type of business I want to go into?

*   Do I have any management and budgeting experience? Or that of cash flow forecasting, marketing, etc; and what have I done to improve my skills and knowledge on these areas?

*   Have I discussed my business/proposals fully with my wife/husband and other members of my family (if any)?

*   Do I receive their support and willingness to share in my aspirations and frustrations?

*   What are their views on what I am planning to do?

*   Will my family be able to survive during the initial months when regular income might be lean? Or when coming home would be late?

*   You really need the support of the members of your family if you are to succeed in your business. Studies on entrepreneurship in many parts of the world show that most successful business people are married and that their spouses provide moral and material support which often help in their success. This is therefore an important **factor that must be considered by you as** you think of or prepare to start your business.

The second activity which you will need to carry out are a set of four tests and they are represented by the word "MIRA ".

"MIRA" is an acronym which stands for, Motivation, Idea, Resources and Ability,

These tests are to confirm and make sure that, you who wants to go into business of your own, has

(i) **The right motivation for going into a business.**

This test will confirm your reason for wanting to go into business of your own. It will ascertain if you are considering going into business because you only want to make money or you have been sacked from your job and you do not have anything to do so you need a survival activity. Going into business of your own with these as your motivation will mean failure.

(ii) The idea is feasible, viable and fits you before creating a business out of it.

(iii) You know **the resources** needed, where and how to acquire them.

(iv) **You have the needed abilities** to produce the product or render the service

TEST FOR THE RIGHT MOTIVATION.

Apart from answering the above questions about the idea you will need to answer some questions concerning your motivation for being in business. Being in the position to answer these questions correctly is key to your success in the business you will start, as this will enable you to have the right reason and mission for being in business so make sure you are able to ascertain that you have the right motivation before you start.

The questions are,

(i)   What do you want to get out of being in business?

(ii)   Why do you want to start your own business ?

Do you want,

Independence?

to earn a lot of money?

power?

to do what you really enjoy?

to serve mankind and bring glory to God?

If your motivation for going into business is to glorify God through rendering true service to your fellow men, become who God made you to be and do, bring improvement to your community and not just to make money for yourself then it can be said that you have the correct business mission and you stand to succeed if you have the skills to run it well.

For the business you start to enable you bring glory to God it must enable you to do the following,

- provide true service to people,

- become who God made you to be,

-do what God created you to do,

- bring improvement to your environment.

True success in business is therefore not measured only by the money being made through the business.

TEST FOR RIGHTNESS OF THE IDEA

For you to be able to create a business which you can enjoy running, truly meet a human need or solve a human problem, is profitable and you can be a success at it, you will need to be able to answer the following questions about the idea;

(a) Does the idea work?

(b) Can you do it/make it/provide it?

(c) Does the idea fit you ?

(d) Will it result in a product or service that is better, cheaper/more readily available than the product/services being rendered?

(e) Is there need for the product or service to warrant its production or provision?

(f) Who will buy it?

(g) Are there many potential customers or

just a few?

(h) Are they local or widely spread?

(i) Who produces/provides the product/service now?

(j) How do you reach the customer?

(k) Will the product/service bring improvement to human life/environment?

TEST FOR THE REQUIRED RESOURCES:

Do you know the

- Equipment
- Labor

- Materials

- Cash,

that you will need?

- Do you know where you can get them?

- What assets do you have already?

These things are key ingredients and you will need them for success in your business. You may not have the four factors in equal proportion as you start a business of your own, but you need a mix of them. For example, someone may have a good idea but very little ability; another may have the ability but no resources, yet someone may have plenty of resources but little motivation.

You can develop these factors over time and get them strengthened in your operations or you can go into partnership with the person or people who have what you lack. You could employ such people if you do not want to go into partnership.

You will also need to gather information about the business you want to start this will help you make projections in the business. While gathering your information you must be conversant with the following factors as they can affect your projections:

(i) Government policies especially the monetary and fiscal policies,

(ii) Consumer demands and tastes.

(iii) Technology available.

TEST FOR THE REQUIRED ABILITY:

What skills have you got?

-are they relevant to your idea?

-are they the technical skills needed for the

 design/making of the product.

-are they the skills that can enable you

manage yourself, create and run the systems necessary for the success of the business you want to start.

Do you know about providing the service or producing the product your business plans to provide?

Do you have the managerial, organizational and resource

management (human and material) skills needed.

-Can you promote/sell your products/services?

-Have you any other help to depend upon like

 wife, father, brother etc.

If you can answer yes to all the above questions then go ahead and create a business by carrying out the next activity which is writing a business plan.

But if you answer no to (k), then find another idea as any business which does not bring about improvement to human life and the community in which it is located should not be started.

WHAT NEXT:

After an honest assessment of yourself, carrying out the tests for motives, resources and abilities and accurately gathering information about your business idea, you will be expected to act and this can be any of the following,

Back-out if you find that, you cannot do the business or the idea is not feasible or viable or both.

Review your proposal by doing any of the following

(a) Create a new business proposal, if your proposal is not viable or feasible.

(b)Change the resources required if the resources you had identified are not adequate

Should any of the above happen, then see it as a welcome development go ahead and carry out the necessary review before proceeding but if none of the above happens and you need to proceed to starting your own business, then the next step you will need to take is to package your old or the new idea into a feasible **BUSINESS PLAN** before starting your business.

You will need to know at this point that a major cause of business failures is the lack of a thoroughly researched business plan. Preparing a business plan helps you spot the defects and potentials of your business idea. A business plan conveys your business goals, the strategies you will use to meet them, potential problems and ways to solve them. Your business plan will also reveal the organizational structure of your business and the amount of capital required to finance it.

A business plan format which enumerates the content of a business plan has been included as part of this publication(Appendix A) for your guide in preparing your business plan.

6:00 HOW TO CREATE THE BUSINESS YOU HAVE FOUND AND SELECTED

A business can be likened to a house as it has the same components as that of a house.

Creating a business or building a business like building a house is about putting in place the components that make up a business. Just as these components must be in place and in good condition for a house to be a strong and good house they must be in place and in good condition for a business to be strong and stands to succeed.

The things that make up the components of a house which must be in place in good condition for a house to be a good and strong house include;

- **A foundation**

- **Walls**

- **Doors and windows**

- **A Roof**

For a business these make up the first set of components that must be in place and in good condition for the business to be strong and can succeed.

For a business,

Its FOUNDATION is made up of its (a)Mission.

The mission of a business reveals why the business exist. It presents what the business is out to do and why it is doing it. For a business to succeed its mission will have to not just be to make money for the owner, it must be about providing a service or a product that meet a need people have.

A business will make money for its owner if it is able to provide people with a service or product that meet a need they have.

You must therefore have and write down clearly a mission which goes beyond making money for your business.

Your mission is an outcome of your motivation for going into a business of your own.

(b) Values/ Ethics, Goals.

The world view of the owner determines these and whether they will be in good condition or not are determined by the owner having and living by a correct worldview.

The WALLS – A business must have walls and they must be solid. They need to be to prevent entry and exit to the business by an authorized people. With walls entry and exit can be controlled and managed.

The walls of a business are its;

BOUNDARIES – These are its means and ways of protection from those that can impact/harm it. Those that can impact/harm a business include,

-the owners direct family members

-relatives

-Friends

-the owner himself

These boundaries must be established and enforced. To enforce these boundaries a business owner must, have a personal budget and must place himself on a salary .Having these will separate him from the business and its resources.

Management – (know your limits).

Purchasing/regulating inventory

Booking-Keeping

Marketing

d. **Personnel;**

Hiring,

Training

Salary /wages

(iii)DOORS/WINDOWS

With the walls in place, entry into your house for both authorized and an authorized people will be impossible. Also with the walls in place nobody can see into your house or out of it when inside. But since you would want others and even you to not only come in and go out but to also see inside your house from outside and to see outside from inside it you will have to provide them/you access, to look into or look out of it and to walk in and walk out.

This is possible only through doors and windows. For a business your doors and windows are the means by which you interact/communicate with others. The means by which you can achieve this include, your,

Marketing

Pricing and costing of your goods (products) and services

Your market (know it)

Your competition (know them)

Your product – what business you are in (what industry/sector of the economy are you in?)

iv A ROOF

Without a good roof, you don't have a house. Things can fall into it and things can fly out. For a business its roof is its **cash flow management**. Having a good cash flow management gives a business a good cover. The components of a good roof(cash flow management) include

Daily money management

Income statements

Expenditure details

You must keep and maintain a good record of the money coming in and going out of your business. For details of records that every business owner must keep please see our book – How to Keep Financial Records for Your Small Business.

Most small businesses and even the big ones fail because of poor financial records keeping.

The second set of components that form aspects a business must have for it to be strong are the following;

Leadership

You must be able to provide yourself and your team leadership. Leadership is needed by you and your team to be able to work together and produce the product or render the service your business is out to provide people.

Ability to provide leadership will enable you to lead your team to achieve your mission

A Team

You cannot do everything that needs to be done in your business to produce your product or service by yourself as you do not know everything and cannot do everything hence you will need people who can work with you to produce the products or render the service that your business is out to provide. These people make up your team.

You must put together your team before you start. If you are not able to do so because of cost which you cannot handle at the beginning then go ahead and start with you as alone as the team member but as you grow consider putting together a team as you can do more working with others.

A product or service – A strong business must have a product or service

A name so that it has a personality (must be a registered entity)

Systems for doing all that you will have to do to produce the product or render the service you are out to produce or render efficiently and profitably.

If you will want more information, personal coaching or a workshop to be organized for your group on how to find, select and build a business successfully, then you can contact,

Efficient Research Dynamic

Jos, Plateau State

NIGERIA

Tel:+234-08107996660,

E-mail, info@erdworld.com or

solomonchikan@gmail.com

APPENDIX A: BUSINESS PLAN FORMAT

COMPONENTS OF A BUSINESS PLAN

A business plan has the following components:

- **COVER PAGE** (Business name, address, phone, email etc)
- **EXECUTIVE SUMMARY** – A short summary of your business who are you, where you are located

What you are selling

Who is you target market

Why will you be successful

Marketing strategies

Management team

How much money will you need

(This should not be more than a page)

- **TABLE OF CONTENTS** (Include page number in contents and on pages of the plan)
- **Business mission**
- **Business goals**
- **History and description of the business**
- **Product or service description**
- **Description of location**
- **Market analysis**

  Industry

  Target market profile

  Competition analysis

- **Market strategy**

Promotional objective and strategies

Pricing

Terms of sale

- **Management team**
- **Resume/CV (for each management staff)**
- **Employee requirements**
- **Income statement**
- **Balance sheet**
- **Financing plan**
- **Supporting documentation** (any relevant information that does not belong in the body of the business plan)

You may place your CV here rather than in the section that deals with management learn.

www.ingramcontent.com/pod-product-compliance
Lightning Source LLC
Chambersburg PA
CBHW071755170526
45167CB00003B/1034